Mastering The Ninja Foodi Smart Xl Grill

Beginners Guide To Amazing Ninja Foodi Smart Xl Grill Recipes For Beginners Who Love Indoor Grilling & Air Frying

Lilla Marcus

Table of Contents

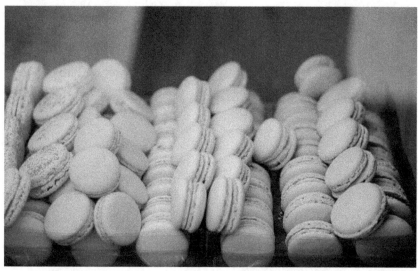

Introduction

N inja Foodi XL Grill Cookbook" introduces you to the Ninja Foodi XL grill and provides you with over 2000 healthy recipes created only for this grill. The book will show you how to prepare a variety of delicious dishes with this versatile grill.

This is the food processor that I have been waiting for since I started cooking. Its large capacity bowl and versatile blade assembly make it an ideal product to use for everyday cooking.

Foodi Smart XL Grill, the latest kitchen appliance by Ninja Foodi, is a food processor that can be used as a griller, slicer, mixer, and blender at homes.

Foodi Smart XL has a large processing bowl of 6.4 quarts capacity that can hold a lot of food for slicing or grilling. The bowl is large enough to make ten servings of coleslaw or salsa, and it is the perfect size for roasting a 3-pound chicken as well.

And the blade assembly can chop, slice shred, mix and blend.

The cookbook starts with an introduction to the Ninja Foodi XL grill. You will learn how to clean the grill, prepare it for use, and then go through the instructions for using this amazing kitchen appliance.

After reading "Ninja Foodi XL Grill Cookbook", you will be ready to make healthy and delicious dishes. You can use this book as a great reference guide for all your grill cooking needs. It can also be a significant learning experience for those who want to get inspired to cook new dishes or gain cooking skills.

When cooking at home, you want a cookbook that delivers. Every cookbook should be tailored to your specific needs, so why not designed for the Ninja Foodi XL Grill? The same team is written by Ninja Foodie XL Grill Cookbook's Ninja Foodie XL Grill Cookbook 1-2-3 series. The Ninja Foodi XL Grill Cookbook offers a practical approach to grilling that will help you get the most from your new grill.

Previous grills have either been too small or not easy to use. I wanted to create the perfect healthy alternative for my family, so I worked on creating a healthier way to cook and grill.

But my mission wasn't only to create a healthy way of cooking but to also make it easy for everyone.

With Ninja Foodi Smart XL Grill everything is easier, and you will be able to enjoy your favorite grilled food with less work and hassle.

While all of our cookbooks provide a great foundation for your grilling adventures, this one is specially designed for this recent addition to the Ninja Foodi XL Grill Cookbook family. We love our Ninja Foodi XL Grill, so we took extra time to make sure we offered the best possible guidance on its proper use.

The Ninja Foodi grill and the other grills differ in several ways. The enormous difference is that the Ninja Foodi Grill heats faster than other grills and cooks much more evenly. This is because the Ninja Foodi Smart XL grill is a solid core-less infrared grill. It uses ceramic infrared burners, which are in a cylinder inside the grill, therefore there are no gaps between the heating elements (unlike most electric grills).

Whether you are a first-time griller or a seasoned pro, The Ninja Foodie XL Grill Cookbook delivers the information you need to ensure that your time spent on the grill will reward and pleasurable.

CHAPTER 1:

Six Methods of Ninja Foodi XL Smart Grill

Now that you have a basic idea of what the Ninja Foodi Smart XL Grill is let's look at the core functions and buttons you should know about. Remember that you have five different cooking types that you can do using your Ninja Foodi Grill.

Grill

At its heart, the Ninja Foodi Smart XL Grill is an indoor grill, so to unlock its full potential, you must understand how the grill function of the appliance works. Let me break it down to you.

Now understand that each set of the Grill is specifically designed for fresh food.

But regardless of which function you choose, the first step for you will always be:

- Place your cooking pot and grill grate in the Ninja Foodi.'
- Let it pre-heat
- Then add your food

The next thing would be to select the Grill function and choose the Grill Temperature. Here you have 4 settings to choose from.

- **Low:** This mode is perfect for bacon and sausages.
- **Medium:** This is perfect for frozen meats or marinated meats.
- **High:** This mode is perfect for steaks, chicken, and burgers.
- **Max:** This is perfect for vegetables, fruits, fresh and frozen seafood, and pizza.

Air Crisp

The Air Crisp mode will help you achieve a very crispy and crunchy golden-brown finish to your food. Using the Air Crisp mode combined with the crisper basket is the perfect combination to cook frozen foods such as french fries, onion rings, and chicken nuggets. Air Crisp is also amazing for Brussels sprouts and other fresh vegetables. Just always shake the crisper basket once or twice to ensure even cooking.

Bake

As mentioned earlier, the Ninja Foodi Smart XL Grill is essentially a mini convection oven. All you need to bake bread, cakes, pies, and other sweet treats is a Cooking Pot and this function. The Pre-heat time for the Bake mode is just 3 minutes.

Roast

The Roast function is used to make everything from slow-roasted pot roast to appetizers to casual sides. Large protein pieces can be put directly in your Ninja Foodi Smart XL Grill and roasted using this function. You can further make this mode more effective by using a Roasting Rack accessory.

Dehydrate

Dehydrators are pretty expensive and take a lot of space in your kitchen. Luckily, you can very easily dehydrate fruits, meats, vegetables, herbs, etc., using just your Ninja Foodi Grill!

The Inspiration Behind This Cookbook

One of my all-time favorite foods is Beef Stew. It's a great meal to batch cook for those busy nights, but it's also what I make for my kids when they're sick. Beef stew is not only hearty and delicious, but it reminds me of my childhood in a way that could bring me to tears. Now, before my Ninja Foodi… Let me tell you how I used to make Beef Stew. First, I would pat dry the beef cubes and season them - this step is a no brainer. Next, I would heat a frying pan on high with some oil and slowly sear the beef, in batches so I didn't overcrowd the pan. It takes a long time and produces a lot of smoke, not to mention, using a lot of oil. Next, I would fill my slow cooker with stock and vegetables. This worked great but took all day to cook and created a lot of dishes to clean.

With the Ninja Foodi, I can sear, simmer, roast, and braise all in one easy-to-clean appliance. The pre-programmed buttons make it so easy, even my kids can make beef stew in it now! This is one of the tabletop appliances on the market that gets hot enough to sear meat properly, so the first thing I made with my Ninja Foodi was beef stew.

What Makes the Ninja Foodi so Great?

Authorization strolls you through how I make beef stew since getting my Ninja Foodi. I open a package of meat, season it, and add it to the Ninja foodi and set it to "sear." In minutes, the temperature has reached 500F so I set a timer after placing the lid on (so there's virtually no smoke at all,) and then come back when the timer has gone off to add the stock and fresh veggies… And voila! In just one hour I have tender, flavorful, juicy, hearty, healthy beef stew!

But it's more than just beef stew! I use my Ninja Foodi for just about everything now, which is why I wanted to create this cookbook (with more than 500 recipes!) to show you how you too can revolutionize the way you cook. You and your family will save time and be healthier in the end - it's really a win-win! (You might also end up feeling like a world-class chef in the end, because everything in this book is so tasty!)

Along with saving money on my energy bill and saving me tons of time around dinner time, this appliance also helped make me and my family healthier! I used to add a lot of oil to the surface of meat before cooking, to prevent it from sticking. I was fed up with losing half a chicken breast on the barbeque so then I started baking them, which didn't offer a lot of flavors. I also used a lot of oil on things like grilled bread, fish, or vegetables. But with the air crisp setting on this machine, you don't need to use any oil whatsoever… which has had an incredible impact on my health. If you're not concerned about oil, this machine will still allow you to enjoy more of the foods that fit into your meal plan – for keto or paleo diets, the Ninja Foodi is a great addition to your kitchen, because of how conveniently you can cook such a variety of proteins.

Making the Most of Your Ninja Foodi

The Ninja Foodi has 6 function buttons which completely replaced my toaster, toaster oven, deep fryer, oven, stovetop, microwave, and even my outdoor barbeque! With this device, I can roast a chicken, a whole fish, or any of my favorite oven meals. I can quickly heat up a piece of pizza or toast. I can air crisp chicken wings or fish sticks for the kids. I can bake a cake or fresh bread. I can dehydrate apple chips or kale chips. I can broil garlic bread or grilled cheese. And probably most impressively… I can grill with no smoke or fire hazards year-round indoors!! Now you try to name an appliance that can do all of that!?!?!

Now you may be wondering – "But is this thing really as good as my barbeque?" The answer is YES and once you try just a few of the recipes from this cook, you will see for yourself. So far, I have grilled everything from shrimp skewers to corn on the cob, to loaded baked potatoes, to hot dogs and yes, even the perfect medium-rare steak. The Ninja Foodi comes with a thermometer probe that is inserted into the center of a seasoned steak, to alert you when it's reached your desire doneness. Once the internal temperature of the steak reaches that temperature, you open the lid and have the perfectly cooked dinner. It really is that easy! Alongside your steak, you can also enjoy perfectly roasted vegetables and potatoes, and you can even enjoy a fresh-baked apple pie for dessert… all from your Ninja Foodi!

One of the finest parts of this machine though is that it reaches a temperature of 500F – this is almost unheard of for a tabletop interior grill. This high temperature allows me to properly sear my food (especially steaks, chicken, or fish) and really allows it to get those tasty grill marks. But this device does more than just sear, as I've told you… because of its unique cyclonic technology, it also circulates the air around your food continuously, which cooks food perfectly, every time.

Ninja Foodi Smart **XL** Grill

Characteristics	Ninja Foodi AG301 Grill	Ninja Foodi Smart XL Grill
Cooking programs	There are five cook programs. Grill, Air crisp, Bake, Roast, and Dehydrate.	There are six cook programs. Broil, Dehydrate, Air crisp, Roast, Bake, and Grill.
Smart temperature probe	Absent. You have to rely a bit on guesswork to attain that perfect doneness.	Dual sensor Present. To continuously monitor the temperature accuracy for even more perfect doneness. Multi-task away since it cancels the need to watch over the food.
Smart cook system	Absent. Requires frequent checks and guesswork for satisfactory results.	Present. With 4 smart protein settings and 9 customizable doneness levels, all the work is done to input the required setting. Just wait for your food to cook. You could be busy doing your laundry while you cook.
Weight	20 pounds	27.5 pounds
Dimension (L×W×H) inches	12.5 ×16.88×10.59 inches.	18.8 x 17.7 x 14 inches. Therefore, this is the larger option for large-sized family dishes and 50% more grilling space.

CHAPTER 2:

Breakfast Recipes

1. Baked Muffin Egg

Preparation Time: 5-10 minutes

Cooking Time: 15 minutes

Servings: 4

Ingredients:

- Parsley, chopped as needed

- Salt and pepper to taste

- 4 large eggs

- 4 large bell peppers, seeded and tops removed

- 4 bacon, sliced, cooked, and chopped

- 1 cup cheddar cheese, shredded

Directions:

1. Take your bell peppers, split cheese, and bacon between them, and crack an egg into each of the bell peppers. Season them with salt and pepper

2. Preheat Ninja Foodi Smart XL by pressing the "AIR CRISP" option and setting it to "390 Degrees F" and timer to 15 min.

3. Let it pre-heat till you hear a toot.

4. Transfer bell pepper to your cooking basket and transfer to Foodi Grill, lock the lid and cook for 10-15 minutes until egg whites are cooked well until the yolks are slightly runny.

5. Remove peppers from the basket and garnish with parsley, serve and enjoy!

Nutrition:

- Calories: 326

- Fat: 23 g

- Saturated Fat: 10 g

- Carbohydrates: 10 g

- Fiber: 2 g

- Sodium: 781 mg

- Protein: 22 g

2. Chicken & Broccoli Quiche

Preparation Time: 15 minutes

Cooking Time: 12 minutes

Servings: 2

Ingredients:

- ½ of frozen ready-made pie crust

- ¼ tablespoon olive oil

- 1 small egg

- 3 tablespoons cheddar cheese, grated

- 1½ tablespoons whipping cream

- Salt and black pepper to taste

- 3 tablespoons boiled broccoli, chopped

- 2 tablespoons cooked chicken, chopped

Directions:

1. Cut 1 (5-inch) round from the pie crust.

2. Arrange the pie crust round in a small pie pan and gently press in the bottom and sides.

3. In a bowl, mix the egg, cheese, cream, salt, and black pepper.

4. Pour the egg mixture over the dough base and top with the broccoli and chicken.

5. Organize the "Crisper Basket" in the pot of Ninja Foodi Grill.

6. Close the Ninja Foodi Grill with lid besides select "Air Crisp".

7. Set the temperature to 390 degrees F to pre-heat.

8. Pick "Start" to pre-heat.

9. When the display shows "Add Food," open the lid and place the pan into the "Crisper Basket".

10. Close the Ninja Foodi Grill with a lid and set the time for 12 minutes.

11. Press "Start/Stop" to cook.

12. When cooking time is completed, press "Start/Stop" to stop cooking and open the lid.

13. Cut into equal-sized wedges and serve.

Nutrition:

- Calories: 197 Fat: 15 g Saturated Fat: 5.9 g

- Carbohydrates: 7.4 g

- Sugar: 0.9 g

- Protein: 8.6 g

3. Breakfast Frittata

Preparation time: 10 minutes

Cooking time: 10 minutes

Servings: 3

Ingredients:

- 1/2 cup Parmesan cheese, grated and divided

- 6 cherry tomatoes, halved

- 1 slice bacon, chopped

- 3 eggs

- Salt and black pepper to taste

- 6 fresh mushrooms, sliced

- 1 tbsp. olive oil

Directions:

1. Press the GRILL button on the Ninja Foodi Smart XL Grill and adjust the time for 10 minutes at MED.

2. Combine bacon, mushrooms, tomatoes, salt, and black pepper in a bowl.

3. Whisk eggs with cheese in another bowl.

4. Add olive oil. Then place the bacon mixture in the Ninja Foodi when it shows ADD FOOD and tops with egg mixture.

5. Grill for 10 minutes, flipping halfway through.

6. Dish out on a platter and serve warm.

Nutrition:

- Calories: 219

- Fat: 14.3 g.

- Saturated Fat: 4.3 g.

- Carbohydrates: 11.5 g.

- Fiber: 3.3 g.

- Sodium: 309 mg.

- Protein: 14.2 g.

4. Cheesy Egg Bake

Preparation time: 10 minutes.

Cooking time: 30 minutes.

Servings: 3

Ingredients:

- 6 slices bacon, chopped

- 6 eggs

- 1/3 cup of coconut milk

- 1/2 cup shredded Cheddar cheese

- Salt and black pepper to taste

- 2 green onion, chopped

Directions:

- Preheat the Ninja Foodi Smart XL by closing the crisping lid and selecting the bake button.

- Set a timer to 5 minutes at 315°F.

- Meanwhile, take a mixing bowl and whisk together all the listed ingredients.

- Generously grease the bottom of the Ninja Foodi baking pan with oil spray.

- Pour the egg mixture into the pan and adjust the pan on top of the rack.

- Put the rack inside Ninja Foodi.

- Close the Ninja Foodi and select bake.

- Set temperature to 300°F for 30 minutes.

- Once done, serve.

Nutrition:

- **Calories:** 472

- **Fat:** 37.3g

- **Carbohydrate:** 3.7g

- **Dietary fibre:** 0.9g

- **Protein:** 30.6g

5. Dehydrated Cinnamon Kale Chips

Preparation time: 30 minutes.

Cooking time: 6 hours.

Servings: 2

Ingredients:

- 1/2 tablespoon cinnamon

- 1 bunch kale

- 1/2 cup raw sunflower seeds

- 1/8 cup sugar

- 1/3 cup water

Directions:

1. Put the sunflower seeds, sugar and cinnamon in a grinder or food processor and pulse.

2. Now add water in small quantities at a time and keep pulsing until the mixture becomes smooth.

3. Thoroughly clean and dry the kale and remove the stems. Then cut or tear the leaves into pieces and place them in a bowl.

4. Pour the cinnamon mixture over the kale in the bowl and toss to coat evenly. Then spread the coated kale over dehydrator trays lined with parchment paper.

5. Turn on the Ninja Foodi Smart XL Grill and press the dehydrate button set to dry at 115°F for 3–6 hours or until the kale chips become crispy. Enjoy!

Nutrition:

- **Calories:** 230

- **Sodium:** 116mg

- **Dietary fiber:** 1.6g

- **Fat:** 17.2g

- **Carbs:** 5.7g

- **Protein:** 14.6g

CHAPTER 3:

Meat Recipes

6. Cheesy Beef Meatballs

Preparation: 5 minutes **Cooking time:** 18 minutes **Servings:** 6

Ingredients:

- 1-pound (454 g) ground beef ½ cup grated Parmesan cheese

- 1 tablespoon minced garlic ½ cup Mozzarella cheese

- 1 teaspoon freshly ground pepper

Directions:

1. Pullout the Crisper Basket and adjust the hood. Choice AIR CRISP set the temperature to 400°F (204°C) and set the time to 18 minutes. Select START/STOP to begin preheating.

2. In a bowl, mix all the ingredients.

3. Roll the meat mixture into 5 generous meatballs. Transfer to the basket. Close the hood and AIR CRISP for 18 minutes.

4. Serve immediately.

Nutrition:

- Calories: 520 Fat: 31 g Saturated Fat: 9 g

- Carbohydrates: 38 g Fiber: 2 g Sodium: 301 mg

- Protein: 41 g

CHAPTER 4:

Fish Recipes

7. Bang Bang Shrimp

Preparation: 5 minutes **Cooking time:** 21 minutes **Servings:** 4

Ingredients:

- 1 cup long-grain white rice 1 cup of water

- 16 ounces frozen popcorn shrimp

- ½ cup mayonnaise ¼ cup sweet chili sauce

- ½ teaspoon Sriracha 2 tablespoons sliced scallions for garnish

Directions:

1. Place the rice and water in the pot and stir to combine. Collect the Pressure Lid, making certain the pressure release valve is in the Seal position. Choose Pressure and fix to High. Fixed the time to 2 minutes, then choose Start/Stop to begin.

2. When pressure cooking is complete, quick release of the pressure by moving the pressure release valve to the vent position removes the lid when the pressure has finished releasing.

3. Place the Reversible Rack inside the pot over the rice, making sure the rack is in the higher position. Place the shrimp on the rack.

4. Close the Crisping Lid. Choice Air Crisp fixed the temperature to 390°F and set the time to 9 minutes. Select Start/Stop to begin.

5. In the meantime, in a medium collaborating bowl, stir together the mayonnaise, sweet chili sauce, and Sriracha to create it.

6. After 5 minutes of Air Crisping time, use tongs to flip the shrimp. Close the lid to resume cooking.

7. After cooking is complete, check for desired crispiness and remove the rack from the pot. Throw the shrimp in the sauce to coat evenly. Plate the rice and shrimp, garnish with the scallions, and serve.

TIP: Use this recipe to make bang-bang chicken: Simply swap out the shrimp for boneless, skinless chicken chopped into 1-inch pieces. Cook for the same time as the shrimp.

Nutrition:

- Calories: 403 Total fat: 12 g Saturated fat: 2 g

- Cholesterol: 178 mg Sodium: 690 mg

- Carbohydrates: 48 g Fiber: 1 g Protein: 26 g

8. Easy BBQ Roast Shrimp

Preparation time: 5–10 minutes

Cooking time: 7 minutes

Servings: 2

Ingredients:

- 1/2 lb. shrimps, large

- 3 tbsp. chipotle in adobo sauce, minced

- 1/2 orange, juiced

- 1/4 cup BBQ sauce

- 1/4 tsp. salt

Directions:

1. Add listed ingredients into a mixing bowl.

2. Mix them well.

3. Keep it aside.

4. Pre-heat Ninja Foodi by pressing the ROAST then setting it to 400°F.

5. Set the timer to 7 min.

6. Let it pre-heat until you catch a beep.

7. Arrange shrimps over Grill Grate and lock the lid.

8. Cook for 7 minutes.

9. Serve and enjoy!

Nutrition:

- Calories: 173

- Fat: 2 g.

- Saturated Fat: 0.5 g.

- Carbohydrates: 21 g.

- Fiber: 2 g.

- Sodium: 1143 mg.

- Protein: 17 g.

9. Spanish Garlic Shrimp

Preparation time: 10 minutes

Cooking time: 10 to 15 minutes

Servings: 4

Ingredients:

- 2 teaspoons minced garlic

- 2 teaspoons lemon juice

- 2 teaspoons olive oil

- ½ to 1 teaspoon crushed red pepper

- 12 ounces (340 g) medium shrimp, deveined, with tails on

- Cooking spray

Directions:

1. In a medium bowl, mix the garlic, lemon juice, olive oil, and crushed red pepper to make a marinade.

2. Add the shrimp and toss to coat in the marinade. Cover with plastic wrap and place the bowl in the refrigerator for 30 minutes.

3. Spray the Crisper Basket lightly with cooking spray.

4. Insert the Crisper Basket and close the hood. Select AIR CRISP, set the temperature to 400°F (204°C), and set the time to 15 minutes. Select START/STOP to preheat.

5. Place the shrimp in the Crisper Basket. Close the hood and AIR CRISP for 5 minutes. Shake the basket and AIR CRISP until the shrimp are cooked through and nicely browned, for an additional 5 to 10 minutes. Cool for 5 minutes before serving.

Nutrition:

- Calories: 246

- Fat: 7.4 g

- Saturated Fat: 4.6 g

- Carbohydrates: 9.4 g

- Fiber: 2.7 g

- Sodium: 353 mg

- Protein: 37.2 g

10. Southern Catfish

Preparation time: 5 min

Cooking time: 13 min

Servings: 4

Ingredients:

- 1 lemon

- 2 pounds catfish fillets

- 1 cup milk

- ½ cup yellow mustard

Cornmeal seasoning mix:

- 2 tablespoons dried parsley flakes

- ½ cup cornmeal

- ¼ cup all-purpose flour

- ¼ teaspoon chili powder

- ¼ teaspoon black pepper

- ¼ teaspoon cayenne pepper

- ½ teaspoon kosher salt

- ¼ teaspoon onion powder

- ¼ teaspoon garlic powder

Directions:

1. Select the "Air Crisp" button on the Ninja Foodi Smart XL Grill and regulate the settings at 400 degrees F for 13 minutes.

2. Mingle the Catfish with milk and lemon juice and let it refrigerate for about 30 minutes.

3. Toss well the cornmeal seasoning ingredients in a bowl.

4. Pat dries the catfish fillets and scrub with mustard.

5. Coat the catfish fillets with cornmeal mixture and arrange the fillets in the Ninja Foodi when it displays "Add Food".

6. Shower with cooking oil and air crisp for about 10 minutes, tossing the fillets in between.

7. Dole out the fillets in a platter and serve warm.

8. Serving Suggestions: Quinoa salad will be a brilliant choice for serving.

9. Variation Tip: Season the fish according to your choice.

Nutrition:

- Calories: 231 Fat: 20.1 g Sat Fat: 2.4 g

- Carbohydrates: 20.1 g Fiber: 0.9 g Sugar: 3.6 g

- Protein: 14.6 g

11.   Mustard Flavored Crispy Cod

Preparation Time: 10 minutes

Cooking Time 10 minutes

Servings: 4

Ingredients:

- 1 large whole egg

- 1 teaspoon Dijon mustard

- 1/2 cup bread crumbs

- 1 pound cod filets

- 1/4 cup all-purpose flour

- 1 tablespoon dried parsley

- 1 teaspoon paprika

- 1/2 teaspoon pepper

Directions:

1. Take fish fillets and slice them into 1 inch wide strips

2. Take a mixing bowl and whisk in eggs, add mustard and combine well

3. Add flour in another bowl

4. Take another bowl and add bread crumbs, dried parsley, paprika, black pepper and combine well

5. Coat strips with flour, then coat with egg mix, coat with crumbs at last

6. Pre-heat Ninja Foodi by pressing the "AIR CRISP" option and setting it to "390 Degrees F" and timer to 10 minutes

7. Let it pre-heat until you hear a beep

8. Arrange strips directly inside basket, lock lid and cook until the timer runs out

9. Serve and enjoy!

Nutrition:

- Calories: 200 kcal

- Carbs: 17 g

- Fat: 4 g

- Protein: 24 g

-

12. Teriyaki Shrimp Skewers

Preparation time: 10 minutes

Cooking time: 6 minutes

Servings: 12 skewered shrimp

Ingredients:

- 1½ tablespoons mirin

- 1½ teaspoons ginger juice

- 1½ tablespoons soy sauce

- 12 large shrimp (about 20 shrimps per pound), peeled and deveined

- 1 large egg

- ¾ cup panko breadcrumbs

- Cooking spray

Directions:

1. Combine the mirin, ginger juice, and soy sauce in a large bowl. Stir to mix well.

2. Dunk the shrimp in the bowl of mirin mixture, then wrap the bowl in plastic and refrigerate for 1 hour to marinate.

3. Insert the Crisper Basket and close the hood. Select AIR CRISP, set the temperature to 400°F (204°C), and set the time to 6 minutes. Select START/STOP to begin preheating.

4. Spritz the Crisper Basket with cooking spray.

5. Run twelve 4-inch skewers through each shrimp.

6. Whisk the egg in the bowl of the marinade to combine well. Pour the breadcrumbs on a plate.

7. Dredge the shrimp skewers in the egg mixture, then shake the excess off and roll over the breadcrumbs to coat well.

8. Arrange the shrimp skewers in the basket and spritz with cooking spray. You need to work in batches to avoid overcrowding.

9. Close the hood and AIR CRISP for 6 minutes or until the shrimp are opaque and firm. Flip the shrimp skewers halfway through. Serve immediately.

Nutrition:

- Calories: 310 Fat: 6.9 g Saturated Fat: 4.1 g

- Carbohydrates: 18.7 g Sugar: 0.9 g Protein: 30.2 g

CHAPTER 5:

Vegetable Recipes

13.   Charred Green Beans with Sesame Seeds

Preparation time: 5 minutes

Cooking time: 8 minutes

Servings: 4

Ingredients:

- 1 tablespoon reduced-sodium soy sauce or tamari

- ½ tablespoon Sriracha sauce

- 4 teaspoons toasted sesame oil, divided

- 12 ounces (340 g) trimmed green beans

- ½ tablespoon toasted sesame seeds

Directions:

1. Insert the Crisper Basket and close the hood. Select AIR CRISP, set the temperature to 375°F (191°C), and set the time to 8 minutes. Select START/STOP to begin preheating.

2. Whisk together the soy sauce, Sriracha sauce, and 1 teaspoon of sesame oil in a small bowl until smooth.

3. Toss the green beans with the remaining sesame oil in a large bowl until evenly coated.

4. Place the green beans in the Crisper Basket in a single layer. You may need to work in batches to avoid overcrowding.

5. Close the hood and AIR CRISP for 8 minutes until the green beans are lightly charred and tender. Shake the basket halfway through the cooking time.

6. Remove from the basket to a platter. Repeat with the remaining green beans.

7. Pour the prepared sauce over the top of green beans and toss well. Serve sprinkled with the toasted sesame seeds.

Nutrition:

- Calories: 200

- Fat: 12 g

- Carb: 16 g

- Proteins: 15 g

14.   Spicy Cabbage

Preparation time: 5 minutes

Cooking time: 7 minutes

Servings: 4

Ingredients:

- 1 head cabbage, sliced into 1-inch-thick ribbons

- 1 tbsp. olive oil

- 1 tsp. garlic powder

- 1 tsp. red pepper flakes

- 1 tsp. salt

- 1 tsp. freshly ground black pepper

Directions:

1. Insert the Crisper Basket and close the lid. Select ROAST, set the temperature to 350°F (177°C), and set the time to 7 minutes. Select START/STOP to preheat.

2. Toss the cabbage with olive oil, garlic powder, red pepper flakes, salt, and pepper in a large mixing bowl until well coated.

3. Arrange the cabbage in the Crisper Basket. Close the hood and ROAST for 7 minutes until crisp. Flip the cabbage with tongs halfway through the cooking time.

4. Remove from the basket to a plate and serve warm.

Nutrition:

- Calories: 400

- Fat: 20 g.

- Saturated Fat: 10 g.

- Carbohydrates: 36 g.

- Fiber: 5 g.

- Sodium: 675 mg.

- Protein: 22 g.

15.   Stuffed Portobello Mushrooms

Preparation time: 15 minutes

Cooking time: 28 minutes

Servings: 4

Ingredients:

- 4 large portobello mushrooms, stems, and gills removed

- 2 tablespoons extra-virgin olive oil

- ½ cup cooked quinoa

- 1 tomato, seeded and diced

- 1 bell pepper, seeded and diced

- ¼ cup Kalamata olives, pitted and chopped

- ½ cup crumbled feta cheese

- Juice of 1 lemon

- ½ teaspoon of sea salt

- ½ teaspoon freshly ground black pepper

- Minced fresh parsley for garnish

Directions:

1. Place the Cook & Crisp Basket in the pot. Close the Crisping Lid. Preheat the unit by selecting Air Crisp, setting the

temperature to 375°F, and setting the time to 5 minutes. Press Start/Stop to begin.

2. Coat the mushrooms with oil. Open the Crisping Lid and arrange the mushrooms, open side up, in a single layer in the preheated Cook & Crisp Basket.

3. Close the Crisping Lid. Select Air Crisp, set the temperature to 375°F and set the time to 20 minutes. Select Start/Stop to begin.

4. In a medium mixing bowl, combine the quinoa, tomato, bell pepper, olives, feta cheese, lemon juice, salt, and black pepper.

5. Open the Crisping Lid and spoon the quinoa mixture evenly into the 4 mushrooms. Close the lid. Select Air Crisp, set the temperature to 350°F and set the time to 8 minutes. Press Start/Stop to begin

6. Garnish with fresh parsley and serve immediately.

Nutrition:

- Calories: 200 Fat: 12 g

- Carb: 16 g Proteins: 15 g

16.   The Veggie Lover's Onion and Tofu

Platter

Preparation time: 8 minutes

Cooking time: 12 minutes

Servings: 4

Ingredients:

- 4 tablespoons butter

- 2 tofu blocks, pressed and cubed into 1-inch pieces

- Salt and pepper to taste

- 1 cup cheddar cheese, grated

- 2 medium onions, sliced

Directions:

1. Take a bowl and add tofu, season with salt and pepper.

2. Set your Foodi to Sauté mode and add butter, let it melt.

3. Add onions and Sauté for 3 minutes. Add seasoned tofu and cook for 2 minutes more.

4. Add cheddar and gently stir.

5. Lock the lid and bring down the Air Crisp mode, let the dish cook on "Air Crisp" mode for 3 minutes at 340 degrees F. Once done, take the dish out, serve and enjoy!

Nutrition:

- Calories: 200

- Fat: 12 g

- Carb: 16 g

- Proteins: 15 g

17.   Amazing Fried Tomatoes

Preparation time: 10 minutes

Cooking time: 5 minutes

Servings: 4

Ingredients:

- 1 green tomato

- 1/4 tablespoon Creole seasoning

- Salt and pepper to taste

- 1/4 cup almond flour

- 1/4 cup buttermilk

- Breadcrumbs as needed

Directions:

1. Pre-heat Ninja Foodi. Press the "AIR CRISP" option and set it to "400 Degrees F" and timer to 5 min.

2. Let it pre-heat until you hear a beep.

3. Add flour to your plate and take another plate and add buttermilk.

4. Cut tomatoes and season with salt and pepper.

5. Make a mix of creole seasoning and crumbs.

6. Take tomato slice and cover with flour, place in buttermilk and then into crumbs.

7. Repeat with all tomatoes.

8. Cook the tomato slices for 5 minutes.

9. Serve with basil and enjoy!

Nutrition:

- Calories: 200

- Carbs: 11 g

- Fat: 12 g

- Protein: 3 g

CHAPTER 6:

Appetizers and Snacks Recipes

18. Chicken and Yogurt Taquitos

Preparation time: 15 minutes

Cooking time: 12 minutes

Servings: 4

Ingredients:

- 1 cup cooked chicken, shredded
- ¼ cup Greek yogurt
- ¼ cup salsa
- 1 cup shredded Mozzarella cheese
- Salt and ground black pepper, to taste
- 4 flour tortillas
- Cooking spray

Directions:

1. Spritz the Crisper Basket with cooking spray.

2. Insert the Crisper Basket and close the hood. Select AIR CRISP, set the temperature to 380°F (193°C), and set the time to 12 minutes. Select START/STOP to begin preheating.

3. Combine all the ingredients, except for the tortillas, in a large bowl. Stir to mix well.

4. **Make the taquitos:** Unfold the tortillas on a clean work surface, then scoop up 2 tablespoons of the chicken mixture in the middle of each tortilla. Roll the tortillas up to wrap the filling.

5. Arrange the taquitos in the basket and spritz with cooking spray.

6. Close the hood and AIR CRISP for 12 minutes or until golden brown and the cheese melts. Flip the taquitos halfway through.

7. Serve immediately.

Nutrition:

- Calories: 444

- Carbs: 26 g

- Fat: 20 g

- Protein: 6 g

19.   Cheesy Shrimp Sandwich

Preparation time: 10 minutes

Cooking time: 5 to 7 minutes

Servings: 4

Ingredients:

- 1¼ cups shredded Colby, Cheddar, or Havarti cheese

- 1 (6-ounce / 170-g) can tiny shrimp, drained

- 3 tablespoons mayonnaise

- 2 tablespoons minced green onion

- 4 slices whole-grain or whole-wheat bread

- 2 tablespoons softened butter

Directions:

1. Insert the Crisper Basket and close the hood. Select AIR CRISP, set the temperature to 400°F (204°C), and set the time to 7 minutes. Select START/STOP to begin preheating.

2. In a medium bowl, combine the cheese, shrimp, mayonnaise, and green onion, and mix well.

3. Spread this mixture on two of the slices of bread. Top with the other slices of bread to make two sandwiches. Spread the sandwiches lightly with butter. Transfer to the basket.

4. Close the hood and AIR CRISP for 5 to 7 minutes, or until the bread is browned and crisp and the cheese is melted.

5. Cut in half and serve warm.

Nutrition:

- Calories: 80

- Carbs: 10 g

- Fat: 4 g

Protein: 0.5 g

20.   Buffalo Chicken Wings

Preparation time: 5 minutes

Cooking time: 15 minutes

Servings: 3

Ingredients:

- 1 tbsp. olive oil

- 1/2 tsp. garlic powder

- Salt and black pepper to taste

- 6 chicken wings

- 1/4 cup red hot sauce

Directions:

1. Select the GRILL button on the Ninja Foodi Smart XL Grill and regulate Medium settings for 15 minutes.

2. Mingle the spicy red sauce, garlic powder, salt, and black pepper in a bowl.

3. Dredge the chicken wings in this spice mixture and shower with the oil.

4. Arrange the chicken wings in the Ninja Foodi when it displays ADD FOOD.

5. Grill for 15 minutes, flipping once in between.

6. Dole out on a plate when grilled completely and serve warm.

Serving suggestions: Serve these Buffalo Chicken Wings with marinara sauce.

Variation tip: You can use fresh garlic, too.

Nutrition:

- Calories: 530

- Fat: 37.9 g.

- Sat. Fat: 12.2 g.

- Carbohydrates: 16.8 g.

- Fiber: 0.5 g.

- Sugar: 5.1 g.

- Protein: 29.4 g.

21.   Butted Up Spinach

Preparation time: 10 minutes

Cooking time: 15 minutes

Servings: 4

Ingredients:

- 2/3 cup Kalamata olives, halved and pitted

- 1 1/2 cups feta cheese, grated

- 4 tbsp. butter

- 2 lbs. spinach, chopped and boiled

- Pepper and salt to taste

- 4 tsp. lemon zest, grated

Directions:

- Take a mixing bowl and add kalamata olives, feta cheese, lemon zest, spinach, butter, salt, pepper and mix well

- Pre-heat Ninja Foodi. Press the AIR CRISP option and setting it to 340°F and timer to 15 minutes.

- Arrange a reversible trivet in the Grill Pan, arrange spinach mixture in a basket and place the basket in the trivet.

- Let them roast until the timer runs out.

- Serve and enjoy!

Nutrition:

- Calories: 250

- Carbohydrates: 8 g.

- Fat: 18 g.

Protein: 10 g

22.   Spicy Sweet Potato Chips

Preparation time: 15 minutes.

Cooking time: 15 minutes.

Servings: 6

Ingredients:

- 2 tablespoons of maple syrup

- 3 large sweet potatoes, to be peeled and cut into 1/4- inch slices

- 2 tablespoons of olive oil

- ¼ teaspoon of cayenne pepper

- Pinch of salt and pepper to taste

Directions:

- Preheat your Ninja Foodi Smart XL to 450°F (230°C). Arrange line a baking sheet with aluminum foil.

- Stir together maple syrup and cayenne pepper in a prepared small bowl. Brush or coat the sweet potato slices with the maple syrup and place them on the already prepared baking sheet. Add pepper and salt to taste.

- Bake in the already preheated oven for 8 minutes, turn the potato slices to the other side and brush with the leftover maple mixture and continue baking until it becomes tender in the middle and crispy edge for 7 minutes.

Nutrition:

- Calories: 252.6

- Carbohydrates: 50.2g

- Protein: 3.6g

- Fat: 4.6g

- Sodium: 125.6mg

23.   Spicy Black Olives

Preparation time: 10 minutes

Cooking time: 5 minutes

Servings: 4

Ingredients:

- 12 ounces (340 g) pitted black extra-large olives

- ¼ cup all-purpose flour

- 1 cup panko breadcrumbs

- 2 teaspoons dried thyme

- 1 teaspoon red pepper flakes

- 1 teaspoon smoked paprika

- 1 egg beaten with 1 tablespoon water

- Vegetable oil for spraying

Directions:

1. Insert the Crisper Basket and close the hood. Select AIR CRISP, set the temperature to 400°F (204°C), and set the time to 5 minutes. Select START/STOP to preheat.

2. Drain the olives and place them on a paper towel-lined plate to dry.

3. Put the flour on a plate. Combine the panko, thyme, red pepper flakes, and paprika on a separate plate. Dip an olive in the flour, shaking off any excess, then coat with egg mixture. Dredge the olive in the panko mixture, pressing to make the crumbs adhere, and place the breaded olive on a platter. Repeat with the remaining olives.

4. Spray the olives with oil and place them in a single layer in the Crisper Basket. Work in batches so as not to overcrowd the basket.

5. Close the hood and AIR CRISP for 5 minutes until the breading is browned and crispy. Serve warm

Nutrition:

- Calories: 327 Fat: 5 g

- Saturated Fat: 0.5 g

- Carbohydrates: 328 g

- Fiber: 2 g

- Sodium: 524 mg

- Protein: 8 g

24. Sweet Potato and Black Bean Burritos

Preparation time: 15 minutes

Cooking time: 1 hour

Servings: 6 burritos

Ingredients:

- 2 sweet potatoes, peeled and cut into a small dice

- 1 tablespoon vegetable oil

- Kosher salt and ground black pepper, to taste

- 6 large flour tortillas

- 1 (16-ounce / 454-g) can refried black beans, divided

- 1½ cups baby spinach, divided

- 6 eggs, scrambled ¾ cup grated Cheddar cheese, divided

- ¼ cup salsa ¼ cup sour cream

- Cooking spray

Directions:

1. Insert the Crisper Basket and close the hood. Select AIR CRISP, set the temperature to 400°F (204°C), and set the time to 10 minutes. Select START/STOP to begin preheating.

2. Put the sweet potatoes in a large bowl, then drizzle with vegetable oil and sprinkle with salt and black pepper. Toss to coat well.

3. Place the sweet potatoes in the basket. Close the hood and AIR CRISP for 10 minutes or until lightly browned. Shake the basket halfway through.

4. Unfold the tortillas on a clean work surface. Divide the black beans, spinach, sweet potatoes, scrambled eggs, and cheese on top of the tortillas.

5. Fold the long side of the tortillas over the filling, then fold in the shorter side to wrap the filling to make the burritos.

6. Work in batches, wrap the burritos in the aluminum foil and put them in the basket.

7. Adjust the temperature to 350°F (177°C). Close the hood and AIR CRISP for 20 minutes. Flip the burritos halfway through.

8. Remove the burritos from the grill and put them back to the grill. Spritz with cooking spray and AIR CRISP for 5 more minutes or until lightly browned. Repeat with remaining burritos.

9. Remove the burritos from the grill and spread with sour cream and salsa. Serve immediately.

Nutrition:

- Calories: 284

- Carbs: 13 g

- Fat: 20 g

- Protein: 15 g

25.   Well Prepped Yogurt Broccoli

Preparation time: 5-10 minutes

Cooking time: 10 minutes

Servings: 4

Ingredients:

- 1-pound broccoli, cut into florets

- 2 tablespoons yogurt

- ¼ teaspoon turmeric powder

- 1 tablespoon chickpea flour

- ¼ teaspoon spice mix

- ½ teaspoon salt

- ½ teaspoon red chili powder

Directions:

1. Wash the broccoli florets thoroughly.

2. Add all ingredients except florets into a mixing bowl.

3. Mix them well.

4. Add florets to the mix.

5. Sit in the fridge for 30 minutes.

6. Take your Ninja Foodi Grill and open the lid.

7. Arrange grill grate and close to the top.

8. Pre-heat Ninja Foodi. Press the "AIR CRISP" option and set it to "390 Degrees F

9. Set your timer for 10 minutes.

10. Let it pre-heat until you hear the beep.

11. Arrange florets over the Grill Basket and lock the lid.

12. Cook for 10 minutes.

13. Serve and enjoy!

Nutrition:

- Calories: 113

- Fat: 2 g

- Saturated Fat: 0 g

- Carbohydrates: 12 g

- Fiber: 4 g

- Sodium: 124 mg

- Protein: 07 g

CHAPTER 7:

Desserts Recipes

26.　　Cherry Choco Bars

Preparation time: 5 minutes

Cooking time: 15 minutes

Servings: 8

Ingredients:

- 2 cups oats

- 2 tablespoons coconut oil

- 1/2 cup almonds, sliced

- 1/2 cup chia seeds

- 1/2 cup dark chocolate, chopped

- 1/2 cup cherries, dried and chopped

- 1/2 cup prunes, pureed

- 1/2 cup quinoa, cooked

- 3/4 cup almond butter

- 1/3 cup honey

- 1/4 teaspoon salt

Directions:

1.　Place the crisper basket and close the hood

2. Pre-heat Ninja Foodi. Press the "AIR CRISP" option and set it to 375 degrees F for 15 min.

3. Take a mixing bowl and combine the oats, chia seeds, almonds, quinoa, cherries, and chocolate

4. Take a saucepan and heat the butter, honey, and coconut oil

5. Pour butter mixture over dry mixture, add salt and prunes

6. Mix until well combined

7. Take a baking dish that fits inside the air fryer

8. Cook for 15 minutes

9. Serve and enjoy!

Nutrition:

- Calories: 330

- Carbs: 35 g

- Fat: 15 g

- Protein: 7 g

27.　　Chocolate Marshmallow Banana

Preparation time: 20 minutes

Cooking time: 12 minutes

Servings: 8

Ingredients:

- 2 bananas, peeled

- 1 cup chocolate chips

- 1 cup mini marshmallows

Directions:

1. Select the GRILL button on the Ninja Foodi Smart XL Grill and regulate MED settings for 5 minutes.

2. Arrange the banana on foil paper and cut it lengthwise, leaving behind the ends.

3. Insert the chocolate chips and marshmallows in the bananas and tightly wrap the foil.

4. Arrange the filled bananas inside the Ninja Foodi when it displays ADD FOOD.

5. Dole out on a platter and unwrap to serve and enjoy.

Serving suggestions: Serve with extra grilled marshmallows on skewers.

Variation tip: Use fresh bananas.

Nutrition:

- Calories: 137

- Fat: 1 g.

- Sat Fat: 0.6 g.

- Carbohydrates: 33.3 g.

- Fiber: 3.3 g.

- Sugar 12 g.

- Protein: 1.6 g.

28.   Ricotta and Lemon Cake

Ricotta and lemon cake can be enjoyed at any time of the day. It is delicious and filling.

Preparation time: 10 minutes.

Cooking time: 70 minutes.

Servings: 4

Ingredients:

- ½ pound of sugar

- 1 orange, peeled and grated

- 8 eggs, beaten

- Butter

- 3 pounds of ricotta cheese

- 1 lemon, peeled and grated

Directions:

- Place the cooking pot into the Ninja Foodi Smart XL Grill and ensure the splatter shield is in position. Close the hood.

- Press the Bake button. Use the default temperature of 380°F and set the time for 40 minutes.

- Press the start/stop button to preheat the appliance for 3 minutes.

- Mix the eggs, cheese, sugar, orange, and lemon zest in a bowl.

- Spread the egg mix in a baking pan and transfer to the Ninja Foodi Smart XL Grill.

- Close the hood.

Serving suggestions: Let it cool before serving.

Preparation and cooking tips: Grease the baking pan with butter before adding the egg mix.

Nutrition:

- Calories: 110

- Fat: 3g

- Carb: 3g

- Proteins: 4g

29.   Easy Muffuletta Sliders with Olives

Preparation time: 10 minutes.

Cooking time: 5–7 minutes. **Servings:** 8

Ingredients:

- ¼ pound (113 grams) thinly sliced deli ham

- ¼ pound (113 grams) thinly sliced pastrami

- 4 ounces (113 grams) low-fat Mozzarella cheese, grated

- 8 slider buns split in half Cooking spray

- 1 tablespoon sesame seeds

Olive mix:

- ½ cup sliced green olives with pimentos

- ¼ cup sliced black olives

- ¼ cup chopped kalamata olives

- 1 teaspoon red wine vinegar

- ¼ teaspoon basil 1/8 teaspoon garlic powder

Directions:

- Insert the Crisper Basket and close the hood. Select bake, set the temperature to 360°F (182°C) and set the time to 7 minutes. Select start/stop to begin preheating.

- Combine all the ingredients for the olive mix in a small bowl and stir well.

- Stir together the ham, pastrami, and cheese in a medium bowl and divide the mixture into 8 equal portions.

- Assemble the sliders: Top each bottom bun with 1 portion of meat and cheese, 2 tablespoons of olive mix, finished by the remaining buns. Lightly spray the tops with cooking spray. Scatter the sesame seeds on top.

- Working in batches, arrange the sliders in the Crisper Basket. Close the hood and bake for 5 to 7 minutes until the cheese melts.

- Transfer to a large plate and repeat with the remaining sliders.

- Serve immediately.

Nutrition:

- **Energy (calories):** 259

- **Protein:** 10.28g

- **Fat:** 18.51g

- **Carbohydrates:** 13.18g

CHAPTER 8:

Main Recipes

30.   Air Fried Teriyaki Chicken

Preparation time: 10 minutes

Cooking time: 22 Minutes

Servings: 3

Ingredients:

- 6 drumsticks, chicken

- 1/3 cup of soy sauce

- 1/4 cup of maple syrup

- 1/3 cup of brown sugar

- 1/3 cup of rice wine vinegar

- 4 cloves of garlic

- 1 inch of ginger garlic paste

- Red chili flakes, to taste

- Salt and black pepper to taste

- 2 cups of water

Directions:

1. Place all the elements in a zip-lock bag and mix well so the drumsticks are coated well with the marinade.

2. Squeeze all the air out from the zip-lock bag.

3. Marinate the chicken for a few hours in the refrigerator.

4. Drain the marinade liquid and then add the chicken to the air fryer basket.

5. Fixed temperature to 400 degrees and cook for 22 minutes.

6. Once done, serve.

Nutrition:

- Calories: 591

% Daily Value*

- Total Fat 24.1 g 31%

- Saturated Fat 6.6 g 33%

- Cholesterol 244mg 81%

- Sodium 1885 mg 82%

- Total Carbohydrate 37.1 g 13%

- Dietary Fiber 0.3 g 1%

- Total Sugars 31.8 g

- Protein 48.1 g

31.   Grilled Broccoli

Preparation: 5–10 minutes **Cooking:** 3 Minutes **Servings:** 1–2

Ingredients:

- 2 cups broccoli, new 1 tbsp. canola oil

- 1 tsp. lemon pepper

Directions:

1. Abode the grill; grate exclusive the unit and close the hood.

2. Preheat the Grill by rotating at elevation for 10 min.

3. Temporarily, blend broccoli with lemon pepper, and canola oil. Throw well to hide the ingredients well.

4. Abode it on a grill grade once enhance food appears.

5. Deadlock the unit and prepare for 3 minutes at MED.

6. Yield out and serve.

Nutrition:

- Calories: 96 Fat: 7.3 g. Saturated Fat: 0.5 g.

- Cholesterol: 0 mg. Sodium: 30 mg.

- Carbohydrates: 6.7 g. Fiber: 2.7 g Sugar: 1.6 g.

- Protein: 2.7 g.

32. Grilled Chicken Legs in Ninja Foodi

Preparation time: 5–10 minutes

Cooking time: 20 minutes

Servings: 3

Ingredients:

- 6 chicken legs

- 2 tbsp. BBQ rubs

- Canola oil spray

Directions:

1. Take a plastic zip-lock bag and spray it with canola oil.

2. Coat the legs with canola oil spray as well.

3. Add the legs to the zip-lock bag and add the rub.

4. Shake it well for fine coating.

5. Pre-heat the Ninja Foodi for 10 minutes at 510°F.

6. Once the add food option appears on display, place the legs inside the grill grate.

7. Close the unit and cook for 20 minutes at MED.

8. One half time pass, open the unit and Flip the less and then glazed the legs with BBQ sauce from both sides.

9. Close the unit and cook for 10 more minutes.

10. Once it's done, serve.

Nutrition:

- Calories: 559

- Fat: 24.8 g.

- Saturated Fat: 6.7 g.

- Cholesterol: 274 mg.

- Sodium: 512 mg.

- Carbohydrates: 0 g.

- Fiber: 0 g.

- Sugar: 0 g.

- Protein: 78.9 g.

33.   Bacon-Wrapped Hot Dogs

Preparation time: 25 minutes.

Cooking time: 15 minutes.

Servings: 8

Ingredients:

- 8 bakery hot dog buns, split and toasted

- 1/4 cup chopped red onion

- 12 bacon strips

- 8 cheese beef hot dogs

- 2 cups sauerkraut, rinsed and well-drained

- Optional condiments: mayonnaise, ketchup or Dijon mustard

Directions:

- Take a large skillet and cook the bacon until it is partially cooked but not crispy, over medium heat. Remove to drain with paper towels, cool slightly and then wrap 1–1/2 bacon strips around each hot dog, securing them with toothpicks as required (do not wrap tightly, or bacon may tear during grilling).

- Preheat the Ninja Foodi Smart XL Grill for 8 minutes before use. Grill while covered over medium heat or Broil. From heat 6 to 8 minutes or until bacon is crisp and hot dogs are heated through, turning frequently. Cast off toothpicks. Serve hot dogs with onion and sauerkraut in buns; top with your choice of condiments.

Nutrition

- Calories 362

- Fat 22g

- Carbs 25g

- Protein 16g

CHAPTER 9:

Sides Recipes

34.   Cheesy Greens Sandwich

Preparation time: 15 minutes

Cooking time: 10 to 13 minutes

Servings: 4

Ingredients:

- 1½ cups chopped mixed greens

- 2 garlic cloves, thinly sliced

- 2 teaspoons olive oil

- 2 slices low-sodium low-fat Swiss cheese

- 4 slices low-sodium whole-wheat bread

- Cooking spray

Directions:

1. Choose AIR CRISP fixed the temperature to 400°F (204°C) and set the time to 5 minutes. Select START/STOP to pre-heat.

2. In a baking pan, mix the greens, garlic, and olive oil. Place the pan directly in the pot. Close the hood and AIR CRISP for 4 to 5 minutes, stirring once, until the vegetables are tender. Drain.

3. Make 2 sandwiches, dividing half of the greens and 1 slice of Swiss cheese between 2 slices of bread. Lightly spray the outsides of the sandwiches with cooking spray. Transfer to the pan.

4. Place the pan directly in the pot. Close the hood and BAKE for 6 to 8 minutes, turning with tongs halfway through, until the bread is toasted and the cheese melts.

5. Cut each sandwich in half and serve.

Nutrition:

- Calories: 432

- Fat: 16 g

- Carb: 20 g

- Proteins: 27 g

35.   Foodi Grilled Cod

Preparation time: 10 minutes

Cooking time: 30 minutes

Servings: 4

Ingredients:

- 2 medium cod fillets, boneless

- 1/2 tsp. ginger, grated

- 1 tsp. peanuts, crushed

- 1 tbsp. light soy sauce

- 2 tsp. garlic powder

Directions:

1. Place the cooking pot into the Ninja Foodi AG301, and position the grill plate with the handles facing up.

2. Ensure the splatter shield is in position. Close the lid.

3. Press the GRILL button. Set the temperature to 350°F and adjust the time to 10 minutes. Press the START/STOP button to pre-heat the appliance for 8 minutes.

4. Season the fish with garlic, soy sauce, and ginger.

5. Transfer to the grill plate and close the lid.

Serving suggestions: Top with peanuts and serve immediately.

Preparation and cooking tips: Flip the items on the grill plate halfway.

Nutrition:

- Calories: 254

- Fat: 10 g

- Carb: 14 g

- Proteins: 23 g

CHAPTER 10:

Poultry Recipes

36.   Crispy Dill Pickle Chicken Wings

Preparation time: 5 minutes

Cooking time: 26 minutes

Servings: 4

Ingredients:

- 2 pounds (907 g) bone-in chicken wings (drumettes and flats)

- 1½ cups dill pickle juice

- 1½ tablespoons vegetable oil

- ½ tablespoon dried dill

- ¾ teaspoon garlic powder Sea salt, to taste

- Freshly ground black pepper, to taste

Directions:

1. Place the chicken wings in a large shallow bowl. Pour the pickle juice over the top, ensuring all of the wings are coated and as submerged as possible. Cover and refrigerate for 2 hours.

2. Insert the Crisper Basket and close the hood. Select AIR CRISP, set the temperature to 390°F (199°C), and set the time to 26 minutes. Select START/STOP to begin preheating.

3. While the unit is preheating, rinse the brined chicken wings under cool water, then pat them dry with a paper towel. Place in a large bowl.

4. In a small bowl, whisk together the oil, dill, garlic powder, salt, and pepper. Drizzle over the wings and toss to fully coat them.

5. When the unit beeps to signify it has preheated, place the wings in the basket, spreading them out evenly. Close the hood and AIR CRISP for 11 minutes.

6. After 11 minutes, flip the wings with tongs. Close the hood and AIR CRISP for 11 minutes more.

7. Check the wings for doneness. Cooking is complete when the internal temperature of the chicken reaches at least 165°F (74°C) on a food thermometer. If needed, AIR CRISP for up to 4 more minutes.

8. Remove the wings from the basket and serve immediately.

Nutrition:

- Calories: 340 Fat: 18 g Carb: 32 g

- Proteins: 18 g

37.   Chicken Potato Bake

Preparation time: 10 minutes.

Cooking time: 25 minutes.

Servings: 4

Ingredients:

- 4 potatoes medium-sized, cut into 3/4" cube

- 1 tablespoon garlic, minced

- 1.5 tablespoons olive oil

- 1/8 teaspoon salt

- 1/8 teaspoon pepper

- 1.5 pounds (680.389 grams) boneless skinless chicken

- 3/4 cup Mozzarella cheese, shredded

Directions:

- Toss chicken and potatoes with all the spices and oil in a baking pan.

- Drizzle the cheese on top of the chicken and potato.

- Press the "power button" of Ninja Foodi Smart XL Grill and turn the dial to select the "bake" mode.

- Press the time button set the cooking time to 25 minutes.

- Now push the temp button and set the temperature to 375°F.

- When it is already preheated, place the baking pan inside and close its lid.

- Serve warm.

Nutrition:

- **Calories:** 695

- **Fat:** 17.5g

- **Cholesterol:** 283mg

- **Sodium:** 355mg

- **Carbs:** 26.4g

- **Fibre:** 1.8g

- **Protein:** 117.4g

38. Lemon Parmesan Chicken

Preparation Time: 10 minutes

Cooking Time: 20 minutes

Servings: 4

- 1 egg

- 2 tablespoons lemon juice

- 2 teaspoons minced garlic

- ½ teaspoon salt

- ½ teaspoon freshly ground black pepper

- 4 boneless, skinless chicken breasts, thin cut

- Olive oil spray

- ½ cup whole-wheat bread crumbs

- ¼ cup grated Parmesan cheese

Directions:

1. In a prepared Medium bowl, whisk together the egg, lemon juice, garlic, salt, and pepper. Add the chicken breasts, cover, and refrigerate for up to 1 hour.

2. In a prepared shallow bowl, combine the bread crumbs and Parmesan cheese.

3. Spray the crisper tray lightly with olive oil spray.

4. Place the crisper tray inside Ninja Foodi Smart XL and select Air fry, set the temperature to 360 °F (182 °C), and set the time to 20 minutes.

5. Remove the chicken breasts from the egg mixture, then dredge them with the bread crumb mixture, and place in the crisper tray in a single layer. Lightly spray the chicken breasts with olive oil spray.

6. Air fry for 8 minutes. Flip the chicken over, lightly spray with olive oil spray, and air fry for an additional 7 to 12 minutes, until the chicken reaches an internal temperature of 165 °F (74 °C).

7. Serve warm.

Nutrition:

-   Calories: 454

-   Protein: 24.99 g

-   Fat: 16.98 g

-   Carbohydrates: 49.11 g

39. Lemony Chicken and Veggie Kebabs

Preparation Time: 15 minutes **Cooking Time:** 14 minutes

Servings: 4

Ingredients:

- 2 tbsp. Plain Greek yogurt ¼ cup extra-virgin olive oil

- 4 lemons juice 1 lemon grated zest

- 4 garlic cloves, minced

- 2 tbsp. Dried oregano

- 1 tsp. sea salt

- ½ tsp. freshly ground black pepper

- 1 pound (454 g) of boneless, skinless chicken breasts cut into 2-inches cubes

- 1 red onion, quartered

- 1 zucchini, sliced

Directions:

1. In a prepared large bowl, whisk together the Greek yogurt, oil, lemon juice, zest, garlic, oregano, salt, and pepper until well combined.

2. Place the chicken and half amount of the marinade into a large resealable plastic bag or container. Move the chicken around to coat evenly. Refrigerate for at least 30 minutes.

3. Insert the grill grate and then close the hood. Select Grill, set the temperature to Medium and set the time to 14 minutes. Select Start/stop to begin preheating.

4. While the unit is preheating, assemble the kebabs by threading the chicken on the wood skewers, alternating with the red onion and zucchini. Ensure the ingredients are pushed almost entirely down to the end of the skewers.

5. When the Ninja Foodi Smart beeps, it has preheated, then place the skewers on the grill grate. Close hood and grill for 10 to 14 minutes, occasionally basting the kebabs with the remaining marinade while cooking.

6. Cooking is completed when the chicken's internal temperature reaches 165 °F (74 °C) on a food thermometer.

Nutrition:

- Calories: 284 Protein: 11.61 g Fat: 12.7 g

- Carbohydrates: 31.83 g

40.   Teriyaki Chicken and Bell Pepper Kebabs

Preparation Time: 15 minutes

Cooking Time: 14 minutes

Servings: 4

Ingredients:

- 1 pound (454 g) of boneless, skinless chicken breasts cut into 2-inches cubes

- 1 cup teriyaki sauce, divided

- 2 green bell peppers, seeded and cut into 1-inch cubes

- 2 cups fresh pineapple, cut into 1-inch cubes

Directions:

1. Place the chicken and ½ cup of teriyaki sauce in a large resealable plastic bag or container. Toss to coat evenly. Refrigerate for at least 30 minutes.

2. Insert the grill grate and then close the hood. Select Grill, set the temperature to Medium, and set the time to 14 minutes. Select Start/stop to begin preheating.

3. While the unit is preheating, assemble the kebabs by threading the chicken onto the wooden skewers, alternating with the peppers and pineapple. Ensure the ingredients are pushed almost entirely down to the end of the skewers.

4. When the Ninja Foodi smart beeps, it has preheated, then place the skewers on the grill grate. Close the hood and grill for 10 to 14 minutes, occasionally basting the kebabs with the remaining ½ cup of teriyaki sauce while cooking.

5. Cooking is completed when the chicken's internal temperature reaches 165 °F (74 °C) on a food thermometer.

Nutrition:

- Calories: 345

- Protein: 15.75 g

- Fat: 6.61 g

- Carbohydrates: 56.58 g

Conclusion

With the Ninja Foodie XL Grill Cookbook, you'll learn how to prepare the freshest food any way you like. You'll start with the basics and work your way up to more advanced techniques. With each technique, you'll get step-by-step instructions and helpful hints to make sure your foods turn out just right. Final Ninja Foodie XL Grill Tips:

- If you're new to grilling, start with the basics—the recipes are written for someone with minimal grilling experience.
- If you're a more advanced griller, feel free to use the recipes as a guide and make your own modifications.
- When you're grilling, always keep in mind that safety is the most important thing—if it seems like a recipe may be too complicated or you're not in a position to grill safely, then don't.
- Remember to grill in moderation and always have plenty of water on hand.
- Don't underestimate your Ninja Foodie XL Grill, especially when grilling.
- Have fun and enjoy the summer!

Tired of bland, boring grilled food? The Ninja Foodie XL Grill Cookbook is the perfect way to kickstart your grilling abilities. With great teaching tools like photos with every recipe and a large variety of recipes that range from basic to advanced and everything in between, you'll be well on your way to becoming a ninja griller.

If you own a Ninja Foodie XL Grill Cookbook, then you already know that it's more than just a grill cookbook. You've probably used it in ways that we never imagined. For instance, you may have used it to make "kabobs" by simply placing the meat on a skewer and cooking it on the grill. That's right! You just placed the meat on a skewer and cooked it!

But there's even more to the Ninja Foodie XL Grill Cookbook than this. You can use the cookbook to start your restaurant using your Ninja Foodie XL Grill Cookbook as a menu. You can even make food for customers right in your kitchen and then have them take it back to their homes with their own Ninja Foodie XL Grill Cookbook. This grill is for everyone no matter if he/she is a professional chef or a person who has just started to cook and wants to cook healthy food with no artificial preservatives added. Ninja Foodi Smart XL Grill is easy to use and will help you prepare your favorite recipes in minutes. It will inspire you to try new recipes as well. This grill comes with an excellent customer support service that will answer any question you might have within 24 hours. A smart grill that promises to cook food faster which is safer and healthier, enter the world of technology. From the name itself, Ninja Foodi Smart XL Grill is a grill that is smart and promises convenient for everyone to use. With this grill, it claims to cook meat in a healthy manner by emitting infrared heat from its dome-shaped lid. It sizzles the meat while leaving moisture and then results in a juicy flavor.

You can also use your Ninja Foodie XL Grill Cookbook to barbecue animals such as turkeys, chickens, and ducks on your grill. And you can roast marshmallows on your grill using your Ninja Foodie XL Grill Cookbook. You'll find all the Ninja Foodie XL Grill Cookbook tools that are necessary to do so inside of this cookbook! In conclusion, if you own a Ninja Foodie XL Grill Cookbook, then you'll see that it's more than just a grill cookbook; it's a tool that will allow you to experience many cooking techniques that we could never have imagined!